GETTING
TO KNOW YOUR
BIBLE

GENESIS EXODUS LEV... | BERS DE... | NOMY JOSHUA JUDGE... | SAMUEL... | S 2 KINGS 1 CHRONICLES
2 CHRONICLES EZRA NEHEM | STHER JOE | MS PROVERBS ECCLESIAS | SONG OF S | EREMIAH
EZEKIEL DANIEL HOSEA JO... | S OBADIAH | H MICAH NAHUM HABAKKU... | HANIAH HA | MALACHI MATTHEW M...
LUKE JOHN ACTS ROMANS | ORINTHIAN | ORINTHIANS GALATIANS E... | SIANS PHI | SIANS 1 T
2 THESSALONIANS 1 TIM... | MOTHY TIT | LEMON HEBREWS JAME... | ER 2 PETER 1 JOHN 2 JO... | JOHN JUDE REVELATION

STEVE PIXLER

STEVE PIXLER

PUBLISHED BY
CONTINUUM MINISTRY RESOURCES
5200 DAVID STRICKLAND RD. FORT WORTH, TX 76119

Published in the United States by
Continuum Ministry Resources
5200 David Strickland Rd.
Fort Worth, TX 76119

Printed in the United States of America

Cover design by Tim Rivers

ISBN13: 978-0-9796261-2-8
ISBN10: 0-9796261-2-9

Library of Congress Control Number:
2011961311

TABLE OF CONTENTS

INTRODUCTION

Without question, the Bible is the most fascinating book in the history of literature. Those who study its pages discover quickly that the Bible is a supernatural and divinely inspired book. It is the record of the good news of our salvation in Christ. The Bible, as we shall see, is very much alive and, as a living book, is so much more than mere literature. The Bible is much more than a literary collection of poetry, history, and biography. It is the amazing story of God's redeeming work in Christ and of our deliverance from the bondage of sin through Him. We must never underestimate the tremendous blessing we received when we were given this written record of God's love toward man. Getting to know the Bible better is quite a privilege. Let's get started!

CHAPTER ONE

LEARNING YOUR WAY AROUND THE BIBLE

If we wish to study the Bible, there are several things we must do. The first thing is fairly simple. First, we must have a Bible. Now, as noted, that seems pretty basic, and yet as you will see, choosing the right Bible for your personal study is an important decision. But for now, whatever Bible you have will do. The super-duper study editions will come later.

Take your Bible and open it at the front to the Table of Contents. You will observe several features that are standard to every Bible. Notice that the Bible has sixty-six books that are divided into two parts called "Testaments" (some Bibles also have a section called "The Apocrypha," but we shall not refer to these books for now). These two parts of the Bible, as you may already know, are called the Old and New Testaments. These may also be referred to as Old and New "Covenants," which is what "testament" means here. The Old Testament tells the story of redemptive history from creation to Christ, and the New Testament tells the story of Christ and the early church through the first century.

The Old Testament contains thirty-nine books that are divided into four sections:

- *The Law* (Five books: Genesis, Exodus, Leviticus, Numbers, Deuteronomy)

- *The History* (Twelve books: Joshua, Judges, Ruth, I & II Samuel, I & II Kings, I & II Chronicles, Ezra, Nehemiah, Esther)

- *The Writings* (Five books: Job, Psalms, Proverbs, Ecclesiastes, Song of Solomon)

- *The Prophets* (Seventeen books, five major prophets and twelve minor prophets: Isaiah, Jeremiah, Lamentations, Ezekiel, Daniel, Hosea, Joel, Amos, Obadiah, Jonah, Micah, Nahum, Habakkuk, Zephaniah, Haggai, Zechariah, Malachi)

The New Testament contains twenty-seven books that are divided into four sections:

- *The Gospels* (Four books: Matthew, Mark, Luke, John)

- *The History* (One book: The Acts of the Apostles)

- *The Epistles* (Twenty-one books: Romans, I & II Corinthians, Galatians, Ephesians, Philippians, Colossians, I & II Thessalonians, I & II Timothy, Titus, Philemon, Hebrews, James, I & II Peter, I, II, & III John, Jude. These are further divided into thirteen Pauline Epistles written by Paul the Apostle and eight General Epistles written by other apostles, James, Peter, John, and Jude)

- *The Prophecy* (One book: The Revelation)

Now, turn to any book of the Bible listed in the Table of Contents. You will see that every book is divided into chapters and verses. This was done by translators to make it easier to find specific scripture references. This makes searching the Scriptures a much simpler task.

The Bible contains 31,173 verses; 1189 chapters; 66 books, written by nearly forty authors in three languages (Hebrew, Aramaic, and Greek) over a period of 1600 years (from ca. 1500BC to ca. 70AD). That is quite a lot of written material, and it is much easier to move around the Bible if we know how to read the chapter and verse divisions efficiently. The Bible is quite a book, and we are grateful for any help we

11

can get in making the task of Bible study a little less complicated.

Looking through the Table of Contents will give you a simple overview of the arrangement and order of the Bible. This helps us familiarize ourselves with the books of the Bible and how to find them.

Much of the preaching you will hear will come from the New Testament, which will become easy to navigate fairly quickly. The Old Testament is generally more difficult for the new Bible student to move around in, but even that will come with time. Don't despair. Everyone had to learn his or her way around the Bible just as you are. It will soon become second nature as you read your Bible daily and follow along with the preaching.

One simple way to follow the reading of the Word in the service is to open your Bible to the Table of Contents, and find the page number of the book from which the minister has announced he will be reading. Locate the chapter and verse specified and read along. You may feel a little slow and awkward at first, but you will soon get the hang of it.

CHAPTER TWO

LEARNING HOW THE BIBLE WAS "MADE"

The book you hold in your hands is a supernatural book communicated and preserved through natural means. The Bible has come to us through an extended process that bears the stamp of divine authorship and guardianship. Yet, God has used finite man to safeguard and transfer an infinite treasure. The preservation of Scripture is truly an amazing story of divine providence.

Here is a simple overview of how we have received our Bible in its present form:

- God spoke to "holy men of God", the prophets, priests, seers, sages, chroniclers, biographers, psalmists, scribes, etc., and they spoke the Word of the Lord to the people of God, the children of Israel.

- The scribes transcribed, or wrote down, what the prophets spoke.

- The scribes then copied and preserved manuscripts of the Word of God, which came to be known as the Scripture, and later, the Bible.

- These original manuscripts, called autographs, were carefully and faithfully copied for distribution and preservation. The scribes had extremely rigorous methods of copying that were employed to retain the integrity of the copies.

- Later, these copies were translated from the original languages into common tongues for everyday use in the synagogues and churches. The Old Testament was written in Hebrew and Aramaic. It is widely accepted that the New Testament was written in Greek, though some scholars argue that portions of the New Testament may have originally been written in Hebrew and Aramaic. The Scriptures were translated into modern languages as the ancient languages fell into disuse and the common people were no longer able to understand the Bible. The story of translation is a long and interesting one that cannot be covered in full detail in this lesson. Suffice it to say, God was abundantly gracious to give us the Bible in our common language.

So, the Bible came to us in three steps:

- *Inspiration*: God spoke to men.
- *Transcription*: faithful men and women wrote it down.
- *Translation*: faithful scholars translated the Word into common languages.

Another important aspect of biblical transmission is the determination of what is called "the canon of Scripture," the sacred writings selected for inclusion in the Bible. The word "canon" originally meant "a reed or a rod for measuring, a ruler." The present order of the Bible was laid out with careful deliberation and discrimination.

The Old Testament canon was carefully determined throughout Israel's history by Jewish priests, prophets, and teachers. The Sanhedrin Council at Jamnia in A.D. 90 officially closed the Jewish canon as it stands today.

The New Testament canon was closed with the writing of the Apocalypse, the Book of Revelation. All of the writings in the New Testament canon were already commonly accepted and widely circulated by that time and were confirmed by several church councils in the ensuing years.

The Bible comes with its own guarantee of authenticity. God has promised us that the Word contained in scripture is divinely inspired. Look at II Timothy 3:16, 17.

> All Scripture is breathed out by God and profitable for teaching, for reproof, for correction, and for training in righteousness, that the man of God may be competent, equipped for every good work.

The Scriptures are "God-breathed." This speaks of the divine authorship of the Bible. The Bible tells us in II Peter 1:21, "For no prophecy was ever produced by the will of man, but men spoke from God as they were carried along by the Holy Spirit." Again, this speaks of the divine authorship of the Bible.

Look at Psalm 12:6, 7: "The words of the LORD are pure words, like silver refined in a furnace on the ground, purified seven times. You, O LORD, will keep them; you will guard us from this generation forever."

This passage speaks of God's intent and promise regarding the perfect preservation of the scriptures "from this generation forever." Forever is a long, long time. It certainly includes our day. The integrity of the scriptures is as sure as the integrity of God Himself. It is the good name of God Himself that is at stake here.

We can rest assured: "the words of the Lord are pure words." God has promised to preserve His Word from *inspiration* to *transcription* to *translation*. We can be confident that our Bible is the divinely inspired Word of God.

CHAPTER THREE

HOW DO WE KNOW THE BIBLE IS TRUE?

People sometimes ask how Christians know that the Bible is true, how we prove that it is not a myth. Well, there are several good answers, a few of which we will consider briefly.

First of all, the *internal evidence* of the Scripture itself is breathtaking when considered as a whole. The Bible possesses an amazing inherent unity, a supernatural coherence. We mentioned a few statistics about the Bible a moment ago: the Bible contains 31,173 verses; 1189 chapters; 66 books, written by nearly forty authors in three languages (Hebrew, Aramaic, and Greek) over a period of 1600 years (from ca. 1500B.C. to ca. A.D. 70). That is an incredible breadth of human history and experience, which makes the internal harmony of the Bible nothing less than astounding.

The entire message of scripture revolves around God's redemption plan in Christ. To get that many—nearly forty—writers, most of whom had never even met each other, to agree on anything is mind-boggling. To have them attain such an organic unity of purpose is nothing short of a miracle.

Another indicator of truthfulness is the fact that the Bible does not "mythologize" its heroes. In other words, the Bible does not present its characters as super-human. If anything, the Bible is embarrassingly honest about the "fleshliness" of the protagonists of Scripture, the actors of Biblical drama.

Also, the writers of Scripture exhibit no personal agenda, no desire for self-promotion, in their writings. What could motivate them to commit themselves to preserving the Bible on such a protracted and grand scale if a force beyond natural motivation did not compel them? Something—or should we say, *Someone*—other than their own desire to appear religious moved them to record the events of the Bible. They were obviously caught up in events bigger than themselves.

The Bible is so plainly real to life, so *natural*, and yet that fact of itself demonstrates the veracity and truthfulness of scripture. It is self-evidently *supernatural*.

In addition to these *internal* proofs, there are many *external* proofs. We cannot cover them in detail, but we can at least mention the witness of archeology, geography, history, etc. The research of the past few centuries has confirmed that the Bible's record of the past is astoundingly accurate. Over and over the critics of the Bible have sought to disprove the Word of God on its historical or geographical details, only to have their research confirm once again that the Bible is right.

Another powerful *external evidence* is the supernatural preservation of scripture. Simply noting the marvelous way God has preserved His Word for every generation inspires profound awe and deep reverence. There have been numerous attempts throughout history to destroy the Bible or to prevent its distribution. And yet, malicious unbelievers have not been able to put out the fire of the Word.

A few examples will suffice:

- King Jehoiakim, an idolatrous king of Judah (one of the tribes of Israel, and the Southern Kingdom after Israel divided in the reign of Reheboam, grandson of King David) tried to destroy the Word by cutting it into pieces with a knife. Jehoiakim is dead and gone, but the Bible is still here (see Jeremiah 36).

- Antiochus Epiphanes, Seleucid king of Assyria, tried to no avail to destroy the Scripture in 170BC.

- The Romans engaged in nearly two hundred years of persecution that failed to stomp out Christianity and its Bible. One example was the persecution under Diocletian, who is said to have heated water with fires kindled with copies of scripture.

- The Council of Toulouse in 1229 forbade possession of a Bible to common folk.

- The Bible—at least the non-Latin variety—made the Pope's list of forbidden books in 1559.

- Henry VIII, King of England, banned common-language Bibles in 1530.

- Queen Mary, sometimes called "Bloody Mary," prohibited the reading or publishing of the Bible in 1553. The penalty for disobedience was beheading or burning at the stake. And yet English, common-language translations continued to flourish.

- In 1778, a French philosopher and writer named Voltaire predicted that Christianity would be extinct in 100 years, and the only Bibles left would be a few copies displayed in museums. A mere *50 years* later, Voltaire was long dead and the Geneva Bible Society was using his house and printing press to publish Bibles that would be distributed worldwide. So much for Voltaire's career as a fortune-teller. Don't quit your day-job, Vol!

Of course, these are just a few of the more notable examples of attempts to prevent the proliferation and distribution of common-language Bibles. Thankfully, all such attempts are destined to fail, for God has promised the supernatural preservation of scripture by His own hand. This miraculous providence is reason enough by itself to believe in the supernatural character of the Bible.

Now, we have considered a few of the *internal* and *external* evidences that confirm the Bible's claim to be divinely inspired. And yet the greatest proof of all is none of the things mentioned before. The greatest proof of the veracity of scripture is the *personal* evidence, the evidence of the truth of scripture in our own lives.

Simply put, we tested the claims of scripture in our lives, and they worked. The promise of the Bible has come true in our lives. For example, the Bible promised us that if we would repent of our sins and be baptized in the name of Jesus Christ, we would receive the gift of the Holy Ghost. We obeyed the command of scripture, and the promise of the Bible came to pass—we received the Holy Ghost just like the Bible said.

There is no greater proof, and when you have experienced the baptism of the Holy Ghost for yourself, you need no greater proof. We have seen it, we have heard it, and we cannot deny it. (Acts 4:20 KJV)

The Bible is somewhat like an old treasure map that has been examined by many critics and declared to be a spurious forgery, only to have someone with simple faith take the chance of believing that the map is genuine and follow the instructions to where "X" marks the spot, where they dig until, lo and behold, they find the treasure.

Now, do you suppose the critics can convince that believer who trusted the map, dug the hole where "X" marked the spot, and is now fabulously wealthy, that the map is a fake? Certainly not. And neither can the critics of our Bible convince us that the Scripture is a myth believed only by credulous simpletons.

We have dug where "X" marks the spot, and we have found the treasure. Furthermore, we are now enjoying spiritual riches beyond our wildest dreams. The critics will just have to find someone else to sell their bill of goods. We have believed, and we have received. This is all the proof of the Bible's veracity that we need. The Bible is right.

CHAPTER FOUR

CHOOSING A BIBLE

New Christians usually want to know about all the different versions of the Bible now available and which one they should choose to use as their Bible. Well, first of all, the Bible teaches us to "test everything; hold fast what is good" (I Thessalonians 5:21). For this reason, among many others, we have traditionally chosen the most widely used English version, the King James Version (KJV; often called the Authorized Version).

The KJV was first commissioned by the English King James I and published in 1611. It has been the world's best selling Bible for several centuries, and it still continues to influence Bible translation. Of course, the language of the

King James is somewhat difficult for those who were not trained to read it from childhood, but once you become familiar with the ancient language and syntax, it is one of the most beautiful literary works in history.

Now, this does not mean that all other versions beside the KJV are inferior. In fact, some of the modern versions are superior to the King James for two reasons.

First, scholars have discovered many manuscripts since 1611 that are older than the manuscripts used in the translation of the KJV and thus tend to give us a more accurate picture of the original texts, which no longer exist.

Second, the modern versions attempt to carry on the KJV tradition of providing the Bible in the common language so that everyday people can read and readily understand the Bible. God has providentially preserved the Bible in everyday language, and the modern versions carry on this work in our generation. The KJV was never intended to become an English equivalent of the old Latin Bibles that ordinary people in the Middle Ages could not read. So, we embrace the idea of rendering the Bible in common language through current translations.

However, though we accept the idea of using modern versions, we must be careful when selecting what modern version to use. Not all modern versions are created equal. We must be careful to choose a version that translates scripture as literally as possible. Some versions use what is called "dynamic equivalence" that translates the general idea of what is said without trying to get it as close to word-for-word as possible. This is an unacceptable way to translate the Bible. We must demand a literal translation.

The modern translation that best suits our need to read scripture in our common tongue while at the same time preserving the need for literal translation is a version called the *English Standard Version,* or the ESV. The ESV is our "official version" of scripture that we use in our public worship services. The ESV deliberately stands in line with the translation heritage of the KJV and preserves its majesty of language while rendering Scripture in a readable manner for modern readers. We highly recommend that all of our members read from both the KJV and the ESV.

One reason for recommending an "official" version of the Bible for our church services as well as our personal devotions is to prevent the inevitable confusion that arises from the use of various renderings that say the same thing in different ways. Uniformity is also good for scripture memorization. Using the same phrasing of the Bible allows us to help one another in confirming the accuracy of scripture quotation.

Once you have decided to read the KJV or the ESV, decide to read it. *Read it!* The best translation in the world

27

does us no good if we do not take the time to read it. Having a Bible written in everyday language helps us only when we read its language every day. Get familiar with the Bible by reading it.

CHAPTER FIVE

HOW TO STUDY THE BIBLE

So far we have discussed:

- The order and arrangement of the Bible
- The inspiration, transcription, and the translation of the Bible
- The integrity and veracity of the Bible
- The modern translations of the Bible.

Now, let's look a little closer at how we can use our Bible in devotions and personal study to strengthen our Christian walk.

Jesus once made the statement, "You search the Scriptures because you think that in them you have eternal life; and it is they that bear witness about me" (John 5:39).

This statement of our Lord outlines for us the best approach to studying the Bible that a Christian can use. Let's examine His statement a little closer to learn how we may know Him better through getting to know our Bible.

First of all, we must "search the scriptures." The only way the Bible can lead us into a closer relationship with Christ is if we will study—or, as Jesus said, "search"—the scriptures. We cannot go into great depth on how to study the Bible within the limited scope of this small book, but we can at least consider a few basics of searching the scriptures.

We will cover five basic study habits for searching the scriptures:

- Make a consistent commitment to study
- Acquire the necessary resources for Bible study
- Develop the necessary skills to search out and understand the meaning of scripture
- Memorize scripture
- Meditate on scripture

Let's look closer at each study habit.

1. *Make a consistent commitment to study*. The first principle of effective study is take the time *study*. Too many learn the

mechanics and methods of study, but never put them into practice. We must commit ourselves to regular study of the Bible.

The best way to do this is to allow your daily devotions to be a springboard to deeper study. You may—in fact, you *will*—encounter scriptures and subjects in the Bible during your daily devotional reading that you will want to search out a little further.

So, start with daily devotional reading. You may want to use a resource such as *Daily Bread*, or *The One-Year Bible* to follow a regular regimen of daily devotional reading. Also, our church follows the *Revised Common Lectionary* readings that create a daily, weekly and yearly schedule of readings that help us read through the Bible over a course of three years. This schedule of readings is published in our weekly bulletin and is emailed daily to all members who subscribe to the church email list. This is a helpful way to read through the Bible.

As you read, keep a journal of your devotions, and when you come across a passage of scripture you wish to search out a little deeper, write it down in your journal so you will remember to look at it later when you have more time. But be sure not to put it off. Procrastination is the greatest enemy of disciplined study.

2. *Acquire the necessary resources for Bible study.* If you are going to be a student of the Word of God, you must invest in

adequate resources to prepare you for the task. Note the following recommendations:

- *Get a good study Bible.* Everyone needs a good study Bible. There are countless editions available, but probably the best starter study Bible is a *Thompson Chain-Reference Study Bible.* It is an excellent study Bible, very easy to use, and an invaluable tool in every Christian's resource library. If you will learn how to follow the chain references through the *Thompson Chain-Reference Study Bible,* you will greatly accelerate your overall familiarity with the Scripture. Other study Bibles will be helpful later on, but, for now, start here.

- *Get a good concordance.* There are several available, but the best for starters is *Strong's Exhaustive Concordance.* This resource will help you look up words to find specific passages of scripture, an essential function when studying the Bible. You may also learn how to use the *Hebrew-Greek Dictionary* included at the back of the *Strong's.* This will become very helpful later on as you dig ever deeper into the Word of God.

- *Additional resources.* You may also wish to obtain a good Bible dictionary (such as *Smith's* or *Easton's*), a Bible encyclopedia (such as *World's* or *Holman's*), as well as investing in some form of Bible software if you have access to a computer. All of this can come later. But for now you may study very effectively with just a study Bible and a good concordance.

- *A journal.* As mentioned earlier, we should develop the practice of journaling while we read. *There is no greater habit to promote study than journaling.* When you make yourself write your thoughts out on paper, or use an electronic means of recording your thoughts, such as a computer or iPad, you clarify your thinking and promote understanding. Every serious student of scripture *must* develop this habit!

3. *Develop the necessary skills to search out and understand the meaning of scripture.* Biblical interpretation on this level is called "exegesis," which is simply a technical term for digging out the meaning of scripture and making certain that we have the proper interpretation. The science, or art, of biblical interpretation is called "hermeneutics."

Again, our space is limited in this lesson, and we cannot teach a full course on hermeneutics, or proper scriptural exegesis. But we can consider a few pointers to help you get started. Listed below is what some call "the eight rules of hermeneutics."

- *Rule of Definition.* We must properly define the words used in Scripture. Our English Bible is a translation of the Hebrew and Greek originals, so we must define the terms on two levels: (1) The English words used to convey the original thought; and (2) the definitions of the original languages with the meaning conveyed in the autographs (original manuscripts). We should use a good English dictionary or lexicon, as well as a trustworthy Hebrew/Greek dictionary. A Webster's Dictionary and a Strong's Exhaustive concordance would be sufficient to get started

- *Rule of Usage.* How did those who heard the word spoken understand the term? The customs and surroundings of Bible times are important to the proper interpretation. This can usually be determined with the aid of a good Bible dictionary or lexicon.

- *Rule of Context.* Scriptures must be understood in light of their setting—what comes before and what comes after? Sometimes meaning can change with usage and context. When you encounter a difficult passage, read the verses before and after to see if you can gain understanding from the context.

- *Rule of Historical Background.* How have the words been interpreted traditionally? This rule must be weighed carefully and used in conjunction with all the others, for the consensus of antiquity can often be nothing more or less than an ancient error. We cannot simply accept the verdict of tradition, though it must be sincerely considered to mitigate and prevent the arrogance of modernity.

  Allowing the fathers to speak is what G. K. Chesterton called "the democracy of the dead." A good Bible encyclopedia is helpful in showing the history of biblical thought on a particular passage.

- *Rule of Logic.* Biblical interpretation is more than mere human logic, and yet it is never illogical. It is much more than pure reason, and yet the message of the Scriptures is not at all unreasonable. The Word of God supersedes these human mental faculties, and yet does not depart from them altogether.

  In other words, though the Bible can only be understood with a spiritual mind, it still makes sense in a common sense way. Proper Bible interpretation will always be Spirit-led and revelatory, yet intelligent and intelligible. It is not necessary to have some strange and mystical twist on the Scriptures to ascertain its meaning. The Bible means exactly what it says. That is, it is not to be interpreted mystically or spiritually.

So, we can approach the Bible with an expectation of a logical presentation of spiritual arguments. Thank God, the Bible makes sense and can be understood by the simple.

- *Rule of Precedent.* The rule of precedent applies in two ways: How was the word or term used the first time it was used? And how has it been commonly used thereafter? A concordance and a good reference Bible should be adequate for this little bit of research.

- *Rule of Unity.* We believe the Bible to be the divinely inspired Word of God; thus, we approach the Bible with a presupposition, an already-settled opinion, concerning the veracity and trustworthiness of Scripture. Therefore, we cannot accept the idea that the Bible contains *inherent* contradictions. If there are contradictions, they are only *apparent* contradictions—that is, they only seem to be contradictions until we have better understood how to explain the supposed discrepancy and resolve the tension. We do not hesitate to say that if the scripture contradicts itself, it is our interpretation that is flawed, not the Bible.

Some would mock our simple trust and childlike faith in the Word of God, but they have not found the treasure. We have the treasure, thus we trust the map. If our explanation of an obscure biblical passage contradicts other plain passages, then we must go back to the drawing board and work out the differences until all the scriptures harmonize. Then, and only then, we have it right.

- *Rule of Inference.* There are some things taught from scripture that are reasonable inferences drawn from settled facts. We do not hesitate to allow scripture to speak implicitly concerning relevant issues that it may not address explicitly. As long as our inferences are consistent with the other rules of interpretation, we may accept them as valid.

4. *Memorize scripture.* We cannot overemphasize the importance of scripture memorization. This is one of the

greatest, and yet one of the most neglected, tools of study available to us. Among the numerous benefits of memorization are:

- *Mental scripture comparison.* As we memorize scripture and thus become increasingly familiar with the Bible, we are able to "run references" on a particular passage in our minds as we study the Word.

  Now, we must always confirm our references to make sure that our quotations are accurate. And yet, this discipline will certainly improve your grasp of overall biblical perspectives on given subjects.

  Be sure to memorize scripture locations (book, chapter, and verse) so you can verify the accuracy of what you have memorized.

- *Greater comprehension during the preaching.* You will find that preachers can sometimes quote a lot of scripture in the course of a sermon, either in part or whole, and your memorization will bring you up to speed with the preaching much faster as you hear scripture used that you recognize and remember.

- *Meditating on scripture.* We will discuss meditating on the Word momentarily, but we must mention here that scripture memorization will tremendously assist you in your devotions as you meditate on the passages you have committed to memory.

- *Victory over sin.* The Psalmist David said, "I have stored up your word in my heart, that I might not sin against you" (Psalm 119:11). You will find that the Word of God will help you overcome and win the victory in your daily battle against the powers of sin and Satan. Quoting scripture and meditating on memorized passages will equip you powerfully to destroy Satan's advances. Try it. You will be amazed at the results.

5. *Meditate on scripture.* There are a lot of folks in the world today who promote meditation in connection with New Age religions, yogi, transcendental meditation, holistic medicine, etc. However, this form of meditation is simply a distortion of a spiritual discipline that has been encouraged by the Word of the Lord since the earliest times.

New Age meditation has one very important and ominous difference from biblical meditation. The meditation that Eastern religions promote is a humanistic, idolatrous meditation that turns the thoughts inward on the self, whereas the meditation of the Bible turns our hearts upward toward God, our Creator. And that is a *huge* difference.

New Agers notwithstanding, we are instructed by the Word of God to meditate on His Law, the Bible, day and night. Look at the following verses:

- *Joshua 1:8* This Book of the Law shall not depart from your mouth, but you shall meditate on it day and night, so that you may be careful to do according to all that is written in it. For then you will make your way prosperous, and then you will have good success.

- *Psalm 1:2* But his delight is in the law of the LORD, and on his law he meditates day and night.

- *Psalm 63:6* When I remember you upon my bed, and meditate on you in the watches of the night;

- *Psalm 77:12* I will ponder all your work, and meditate on your mighty deeds.

- *Psalm 119:48* I will lift up my hands toward your commandments, which I love, and I will meditate on your statutes.

- *1 Timothy 4:15* Practice (Meditate) these things, immerse yourself in them, so that all may see your progress. (comments added)

So, we are instructed to meditate on the Word of God. How do we meditate scripturally? By starting with the habits of effective study listed above. We meditate effectively simply by reading the Bible, seeking to understand its meaning, and then thinking on what we have read. This is where we make personal application of the scripture and pray the Word into our heart. This is also where scripture memorization plays such a vital role.

We should incorporate Bible meditation into our morning devotions, which should consist of prayer, Bible reading, and meditation. As we go through the day, we should seek to recall what we read that morning and try to apply it to our lives throughout the day.

Again, this is where memorization is so important. Write your daily scripture down on a 3x5 index card and refer to it occasionally when you can to help you memorize the Word. Then, as you go through the day, meditate on the Word. This will give you such an edge in your walk with God. Give it a try and you will notice the difference immediately.

So, to review what we have covered, we must learn at least these five basics for "searching the scriptures":

1) Make a consistent commitment to study; 2) acquire the necessary resources for Bible study; 3) develop the necessary skills to search out and understand the meaning of scripture; 4) memorize scripture; and 5) meditate on scripture.

If you will make the commitment to pursue these things, you will have gained a tremendous head start on discipleship. You will quickly become proficient and accomplished in studying the Bible, searching the scriptures, which will provide a distinct advantage for you in your Christian experience.

CHAPTER SIX

LEARNING TO "THINK RIGHT"

Now let's return to the statement of Jesus in John 5:39. "You search the Scriptures because you think that in them you have eternal life; and it is they that bear witness about me"

We have discussed "search the scriptures," and the principles of studying the Scriptures. Now, let's look at the second part of the statement "because you think that in them you have eternal life."

Jesus' statement here was made to a group of religious hypocrites, the Pharisees, who professed that they knew and obeyed the Scriptures. And yet, when Christ came as the promised Messiah of whom the Scriptures had spoken, they refused to recognize the Lord for who He was. They professed to know and obey the Scriptures, yet they rejected the very God of the Bible manifest in Christ, the Son of God.

So, Jesus said to them, "You search the Scriptures because you think that in them you have eternal life; and it is they that bear witness about me" *Because you think that in them you have eternal life.* Strong words, indeed!

Jesus points out the disturbing reality that a man may give his life to searching the scriptures, thinking that he has found eternal life therein, only to miss the true message of the Word of God and end up deceived. This should be a sobering thought for every serious student of scripture.

This highlights the fact that we must do more than simply "search the scriptures." We must "think" right as we search the scriptures. In other words, the attitude and spirit with which we approach the Word of God make all the difference in the world.

How are we thinking as we search the Scriptures? That is the question. Do we have an open mind? Are we studying with humility? Do we think we have eternal life, that we have it all figured out, and that we do not need a deeper understanding of the Scripture? This is certainly how the Pharisees thought. We must stop and ask ourselves these questions as we begin to study the Word of God. Are we thinking right?

First of all, we must recognize that we can know nothing except what the Holy Ghost teaches us. An honest recognition of this fact alone will serve to keep us truly humble as we open our Bible. The truth of God's Word can only be known by revelation. It is impossible to learn anything about God that He does not graciously reveal to us by His own initiative. We can know nothing of our selves. Consider the following scriptures:

- *Matthew 11:25-27* At that time Jesus declared, "I thank you, Father, Lord of heaven and earth, that you have hidden these things from the wise and understanding and revealed them to little children; yes, Father, for such was your gracious will. All things have been handed over to me by my Father, and no one knows the Son except the Father, and no one knows the Father except the Son and anyone to whom the Son chooses to reveal him."

- *Matthew 16:13-20* Now when Jesus came into the district of Caesarea Philippi, he asked his disciples, "Who do people say that the Son of Man is?" And they said, "Some say John the Baptist, others say Elijah, and others Jeremiah or one of the prophets." He said to them, "But who do you say that I am?" Simon Peter replied, "You are the Christ, the Son of the living God." And Jesus answered him, "Blessed are you, Simon Bar-Jonah! For flesh and blood has not revealed this to you, but my Father who is in heaven. And I tell you, you are Peter, and on this rock I will build my church, and the gates of hell shall not prevail against it. I will give you the keys of the kingdom of heaven, and whatever you bind on earth shall be bound in heaven, and whatever you loose on earth shall be loosed in heaven." Then he strictly charged the disciples to tell no one that he was the Christ.

- *Isaiah 54:13* All your children shall be taught by the LORD, and great shall be the peace of your children.

- *John 6:45* It is written in the Prophets, "And they will all be taught by God." Everyone who has heard and learned from the Father comes to me.

- *I Corinthians 2:9-12* But, as it is written, "What no eye has seen, nor ear heard, nor the heart of man imagined, what God has prepared for those who love him." - these things God has revealed to us through the Spirit. For the Spirit searches

LEARNING TO "THINK RIGHT"

everything, even the depths of God. For who knows a person's thoughts except the spirit of that person, which is in him? So also no one comprehends the thoughts of God except the Spirit of God. Now we have received not the spirit of the world, but the Spirit who is from God, that we might understand the things freely given us by God.

- *Ephesians 1:17* That the God of our Lord Jesus Christ, the Father of glory, may give you a spirit of wisdom and of revelation in the knowledge of him.

- *Ephesians 3:4, 5* When you read this, you can perceive my insight into the mystery of Christ, which was not made known to the sons of men in other generations as it has now been revealed to his holy apostles and prophets by the Spirit.

- *Ephesians 3:18, 19* May have strength to comprehend with all the saints what is the breadth and length and height and depth, and to know the love of Christ that surpasses knowledge, that you may be filled with all the fullness of God.

- *Colossians 1:26, 27* The mystery hidden for ages and generations but now revealed to his saints.

To them God chose to make known how great among the Gentiles are the riches of the glory of this mystery, which is Christ in you, the hope of glory.

- *I John 5:20* And we know that the Son of God has come and has given us understanding, so that we may know him who is true; and we are in him who is true, in his Son Jesus Christ. He is the true God and eternal life.

We must receive the "spirit of wisdom and revelation" in order to understand the Word of God. We are blinded by sin and unbelief until the grace of God comes and opens our eyes to understand the Word of God. Take a moment to read carefully the following passage of scripture. Slow down and think on the words as you read.

Since we have such a hope, we are very bold, not like Moses, who would put a veil over his face so that the Israelites might not gaze at the outcome of what was being brought to an end. But their minds were hardened. For to this day, when they read the old covenant, that same veil remains unlifted, because only through Christ is it taken away. Yes, to this day whenever Moses is read a veil lies over their hearts. But when one turns to the Lord, the veil is removed.

Now the Lord is the Spirit, and where the Spirit of the Lord is, there is freedom. And we all, with unveiled face, beholding the glory of the Lord, are being transformed into the same image from one degree of glory to another. For this comes from the Lord who is the Spirit. Therefore, having this ministry by the mercy of God, we do not lose heart. But we have renounced disgraceful, underhanded ways. We refuse to practice cunning or to tamper with God's word, but by the open statement of the truth we would commend ourselves to everyone's conscience in the sight of God. And even if our gospel is veiled, it is veiled only to those who are perishing. In their case the god of this world has blinded the minds of the unbelievers, to keep them from seeing the light of the gospel of the glory of Christ, who is the image of God. (II Corinthians 3:12-4:4)

Notice the last verse of this passage:

In their case the god of this world has blinded the minds of the unbelievers, to keep them from seeing the light of the gospel of the glory of Christ, who is the image of God.

This verse describes the blinded state that Satan has inflicted on sinners through their unbelief. This was the spiritual condition of every one of us before the grace of God came and opened our eyes to believe the gospel and understand the scriptures. We cannot understand the Bible unless the Holy Spirit opens our eyes to see.

Read and meditate on the following scriptures concerning God opening the "eyes of our heart" that we may understand the Word of God:

- *Psalm 119:18* Open my eyes, that I may behold wondrous things out of your law.

- *Luke 24:44-48* Then he said to them, "These are my words that I spoke to you while I was still with you, that everything written about me in the Law of Moses and the Prophets and the Psalms must be fulfilled." Then he opened their minds to understand the Scriptures, and said to them, "Thus it is written, that the Christ should suffer and on the third day rise from the dead, and that repentance and forgiveness of sins should be proclaimed in his name to all nations, beginning from Jerusalem. You are witnesses of these things."

- *Acts 16:14* One who heard us was a woman named Lydia, from the city of Thyatira, a seller of purple goods, who was a worshiper of God. The

Lord opened her heart to pay attention to what was said by Paul.

- *Acts 26:18* To open their eyes, so that they may turn from darkness to light and from the power of Satan to God, that they may receive forgiveness of sins and a place among those who are sanctified by faith in me.

- *Ephesians 1:17-23* That the God of our Lord Jesus Christ, the Father of glory, may give you a spirit of wisdom and of revelation in the knowledge of him, having the eyes of your hearts enlightened, that you may know what is the hope to which he has called you, what are the riches of his glorious inheritance in the saints, and what is the immeasurable greatness of his power toward us who believe, according to the working of his great might that he worked in Christ when he raised him from the dead and seated him at his right hand in the heavenly places, far above all rule and authority and power and dominion, and above every name that is named, not only in this age but also in the one to come. And he put all things under his feet and gave him as head over all things to the church, which is his body, the fullness of him who fills all in all.

All of these scriptures teach us of the importance of thinking right as we search the scriptures. We must approach the Bible with a humility born of a revelation-realization: the realization that we can know *nothing* about God except He graciously reveals it to us.

Jesus charges the Pharisees with thinking smugly, and yet, thinking *wrongly*, that they possessed eternal life through the scriptures that they had so carefully studied. They were blinded to the truth right before their eyes through their own unbelief and pride. His words should warn us today.

We cannot say it forcefully enough: when we become wise in our own conceits and through pride begin to resist the teaching of the Word of the Lord in favor of our own studied and hardened opinions, then we will inevitably become spiritual casualties to Satan through blindness and unbelief.

This does not mean that we should not search the scriptures eagerly to know the truth. Rather, it means that we must be careful that we approach the Bible with the right spirit and with right thinking. Question? Yes. But question right.

The proper mindset that students of the Bible must possess as they begin to search the scriptures can be summed up in three words: *hunger, humility,* and *honesty*. Passionate, driving hunger. Simple, unadorned humility. Transparent, straightforward honesty. Think about these things. Hunger, humility, and honesty. Is this how you study the Word?

True humility is rooted in a deep spiritual hunger, and true humility will always bear the abundant fruit of honesty. Those who hunger deeply after God are not interested in proudly defending their personal opinions or doctrinal positions against the clear teaching of scripture. Rather, they are anxious to learn everything they can at the foot of the Master.

This was the problem with the Pharisees in John 5:39. They were not hungry for the truth, thus they did not possess the humility to acknowledge the truth. They were not hungry, humble and honest. They were blinded by their own pride and unbelief.

This is a trap that every Christian disciple must avoid at all costs. Stay hungry, stay humble, and stay honest.

Jesus said in Matthew 5:6, "Blessed are those who hunger and thirst for righteousness, for they shall be satisfied."

This is an explicit promise. Those who hunger and thirst shall be satisfied. If we hunger for righteousness, for truth, for godliness, God guarantees us that we shall receive according to our hunger. This is our assurance. As we truly and faithfully search the scriptures, we will know—not just *think*—but we will *know*, that we have eternal life.

Is it indeed possible to know with such resolute certainty that we have eternal life? Absolutely. We can and we must. The key to this assurance is confidence in the trustworthiness of God's promise: the hungry shall be filled.

Now, the question is, Are you genuinely hungry? If you are, then you can be certain that your search for eternal life in the Word of God will be rewarded.

We refuse to imitate the Pharisees, who deceived themselves through pride and unbelief into thinking that their studies had discovered truth, only to be exposed by Jesus as shallow hypocrites who lacked a real hunger for true righteousness. We are hungry, humble, and honest, and therefore, we *know* that we have eternal life.

CHAPTER SEVEN

GETTING TO KNOW JESUS

In conclusion, let's go back one final time to the statement of Jesus in John 5:39. "You search the Scriptures because you think that in them you have eternal life; and it is they that bear witness about me."

We have discussed the principles of studying, or searching, the Word of God. We have considered studying the Bible with right thinking, with a revelation-realization, and with hunger, humility, and honesty. Now, look briefly at the third part of Jesus' statement, "And it is they that bear witness about me."

The entire message of scripture revolves around God's redemption plan in Christ. It could be said that the Bible is a beautiful portrait of Christ. The outlines of the life and ministry of Christ from the First Advent, His birth in Bethlehem, to the Second Advent, when He shall return to judge the world and reign in the fullness of His Kingdom, are set forth in scripture. All Scripture testifies of Him.

Therefore, getting to know your Bible is all about getting to know Jesus Christ, for He is the central character, the message and the meaning of the Word of God. In fact, He *is* the Word of God, the Living Word made flesh in Christ Jesus. (John 1:1)

As we get to know the Bible, as the spirit of wisdom and revelation unveils the image of Christ in the scripture, we will gain a greater and deeper relationship with the Lord. Revelation brings relationship. This is the ultimate purpose for studying the Bible—to know more about our Lord and Savior, Jesus Christ. We do not study simply for intellectual expertise, or for academic prowess. We study to know *Him.*

Search the scriptures. Study the Bible. *Think right as you study.* The proper attitude of hunger, humility, and honesty will give you the assurance that you have eternal life through the scriptures. *And the scriptures will testify of Jesus Christ.* You will gain a deeper relationship with the Lord Jesus as you study. This is reason enough and reward enough for diligent study. We have a deep desire to know Him and love Him, which is why we are becoming disciples of Jesus Christ.

We must make the Bible our closest friend and constant companion, for it is more than just the story of Jesus Christ. It is the living Christ revealed in scripture.

Consider one final scripture.

> For the word of God is living and active, sharper than any two-edged sword, piercing to the division of soul and of spirit, of joints and of marrow, and discerning the thoughts and intentions of the heart. (Hebrews 4:12)

The Word of God is "alive," and powerful. It pierces into the depths of our heart and soul. Never take the Bible for granted. It is a supernatural book.

As you continue getting to know your Bible, you will be confronted with demands and expectations written in the Word of God that may seem unusual and even unreasonable to the carnal mind. It is then that our attitude and conviction concerning scripture will be truly manifested. Do we really believe that the Bible is the Word of God and contains God's revealed will that we must follow?

If we truly believe that the Bible is the revealed Word of God, then we will humbly obey. The only question for the sincere Bible student is what does the Bible say? Once that is determined, it simply becomes a matter of obedience. Let's get to know our Bible, and the Christ of our Bible, better.